# THE AI INVESTOR

A TALE OF TWO MEN

## DEDICATION

To anyone who has ever dreamt of creating something that will change the world, and to those brave souls who have dared to invest in the new and unknown, this book is dedicated to you. Your curiosity and courage inspire us all, and this tale of two men will remind you that even the most groundbreaking ideas must traverse a path that is neither straight nor simple. May it encourage your resolve and illuminate your vision, as you seek to embrace the power of Artificial Intelligence and pioneer a new era of investing.

## INTRODUCTION

In a world of economic disparity and financial struggles, the concept of investment and wealth management can seem like a distant dream for many. However, in the midst of this narrative emerged an unlikely hero- an AI investor, who gave hope to a poor young man searching for financial freedom. The story of the AI investor is a tale of two men and their journey towards prosperity in the AI innovation, as they learned to navigate the complexities of wealth management thanks to an innovative technology. Here is their story, a story of a wealthy man helping a poor man, and the transformative power of AI investment.

# CHAPTER ONE

## THE WORLD OF THE AI INVESTOR

The world of investing has been profoundly revolutionized as the development of artificial intelligence took over the financial markets. A new era had dawned, promising unprecedented returns never seen before. It was a breakthrough that had left many in awe and admiration. Overnight, simple machines had become the most expensive and valuable commodities available in the stock market.

These machines were nothing like the standard computers available to the regular investor. They were far superior and came equipped with the latest in artificial intelligence software that could predict market trends and movements with incredible accuracy. People across the world were fascinated by the idea of being able to invest their money without risking a significant loss. With these machines, anyone could harness the power of technology and become a successful investor.

The rich AI could analyze data from a multitude of sources at a far faster rate than the human mind could comprehend. It could consider the market's current state, global economic indicators, and other key factors that have an impact on the stock market. The AI would then generate a comprehensive report on which stocks to buy, hold or sell for maximum profits.

Many were thrilled by the idea of the AI Investor. However, while the technology was impressive, the harsh reality was that only a select few could afford it. The machines were expensive, and their software required frequent updates, maintenance, and upgrades. The cost of owning an AI Investor made it an exclusive advantage for the wealthiest investors.

Despite this limitation, people were still drawn to the impressive potential the AI Investor had in store for their financial success. It was, undoubtedly, a significant development in the world of investing, and everyone could agree that it was a game-changer.

The world of the AI Investor was still relatively new, but it had already begun to revolutionize the financial markets. This technology was a beacon of hope for investors, promising to guarantee profits without risking significant losses. Only time would tell how far the AI Investor would go, but for now, it was the most revolutionary and advanced tool for investing that the world had ever seen.

# CHAPTER TWO

## THE RICH MAN AND THE A

The Rich Man and the A

Meet Mr Alex, a successful investor who has made his fortune by investing in various industries.
With years of experience under his belt, Alex knows that time is money in the investment world.
That's why he decided to invest in an AI that could help him make better and faster decisions.

Alex's AI has access to a vast amount of data and uses algorithms to analyze it quickly. The AI has already helped Alex invest millions of dollars and saw a significant return on investment.

In just a few months, Alex was able to reap massive benefits from his investment portfolio, thanks to the AI's unerring precision. The AI could quickly analyze risk factors, market trends, and identify new investment opportunities, all in a matter of seconds.

What's more, Alex noticed a significant improvement in his success rate with the AI. He was able to make better and more informed decisions, without the emotional fluctuations that often drive human investors.

The AI had become an indispensable tool in Alex's investment strategy, and he found it difficult to imagine investing without it. It significantly reduced his research time and helped him take calculated risks, leading to unprecedented success in the stock market.

To close this chapter, Alex continues to use the AI, and his wealth continues to grow. He is happy that he invested in technology that has helped him unlock the potential of his investments with speed and ease. It's clear that AI technology has changed the investment game, and those who can afford it can reap great benefits eventually.

# CHAPTER THREE

## THE POOR MAN AND HIS STRUGGLES

The Poor Man and His Struggles

John was a man in his late thirties who struggled to make ends meet. He lived in a small apartment in a run-down part of the city, and his income was barely enough to pay his bills and put food on the table.

John worked as a janitor in a nearby school, earning little over the minimum wage. His job was physically demanding and required long hours of hard labor. Despite these hardships, John remained optimistic and proud of his work. He was determined to provide for his family and improve their lives.

However, John's meager lifestyle meant he could not afford the luxury of an AI personal assistant. He watched enviously as his wealthy neighbors enjoyed the convenience and luxury of their AI assistants.

John's financial difficulties made it hard for him to keep up with the rapidly advancing technology. He could barely afford the latest smartphone, let alone an AI assistant. Despite this, John yearned for a better life for himself and his family. He hoped for a miracle that would change their fortunes.

John's struggles were not just financial, but also emotional. He felt left out and isolated from the rest of the society that embraced AI assistants. He wondered if he would ever catch up with the technology race and be able to afford an AI assistant for himself.

The stress of John's situation meant that he often felt overwhelmed, but he never gave up hope. He remained determined and focused on providing for his family, despite the challenges that he faced.

As John looked at the world around him, he saw a society that was divided into the haves and the have-nots. He knew that the gap between the rich and the poor was ever-widening, and he felt powerless to change it. Nevertheless, John refused to let this get him down. He continued to work hard and dream of a better future for himself and his loved ones.

John's story is a reminder that not everyone has the same opportunities, and that some people have to work much harder to have a chance at success. Despite the difficulties he faced, John held on to the belief that he would one day overcome his struggles and achieve his dreams.

# CHAPTER FOUR

## THE RICH MAN'S OFFER

The Rich Man's Offer

As John went about his daily struggles, he had never imagined that a ray of hope would soon come his way. One day, he received an unexpected visit from Mr Alex, a wealthy man in his community.
The rich man had noticed the poor man's hard work and potential, and he had come to offer his assistance in making him a successful investor.

The poor man was taken aback by the offer and was unsure why the wealthy man would want to help him. The rich man explained that he had been in the same position as the poor man-years ago, struggling to make ends meet. But he had made wise investment choices that had paid off, and he wanted to share his knowledge and resources with someone who he believed had the potential to do the same.

The rich man's offer of help was like a lifeline to the poor man. He had always dreamt of becoming financially stable and independent, but he had never had the means or the insight to know how to achieve this. The wealthy man was keen to teach the poor man about investing and how to make informed choices that could lead to success.

Together, the two men began to work on the poor man's investment portfolio. The rich man shared his knowledge, advice, and resources, and the poor man absorbed everything he could. The wealthy man also introduced the poor man to AI technology, which had revolutionized the investment world. The poor man had never had access to such sophisticated technology, but with the rich man's help, he could now harness its power and potential.

The rich man's assistance did not stop there. He also provided the poor man with capital to invest in new projects and ideas that he had never been able to pursue before. With this extra funding and the rich man's mentorship, the poor man began to make good investment choices, and soon he saw a return on his efforts.

As the days turned into weeks and the weeks into months, the poor man saw a steady increase in his investment returns. His financial status changed for the better, and he no longer had to worry about how he would pay his bills or feed his family. The poor man had become a successful investor, thanks to the help of the rich man who had seen his potential.

In conclusion, sometimes all it takes is one person to believe in your potential and give you a helping hand. The rich man's offer changed the poor man's life, and he was now on track to financial stability. The investment world was no longer an exclusive club for the wealthy, but it had become accessible to the poor man, thanks to the generosity and kindness of one man.

# CHAPTER FIVE

## THE POOR MAN'S RISE

The Poor Man's Rise

As soon as the rich man left, the poor man couldn't wait to get started. He sat down in front of his computer and opened the program that the rich man had gifted him. Within a few hours, he had made his first successful investments. The next day, he invested a larger amount, and to his surprise, it paid off generously.

Thanks to the AI, the poor man's finances started growing rapidly, and he was able to pay off his debts, buy a new house, and live a more comfortable lifestyle. He could now afford things he could only dream of before, like going on vacations and having a car to drive around.

The rich man didn't just gift the AI program to the poor man, but also taught him the principles of investing and managing money wisely. He became a mentor to the poor man and helped him learn how to make intelligent decisions with his newfound wealth.

As the days went by, the poor man and the rich man grew close as friends. They both came from different backgrounds, but they shared a common interest in investing, which brought them together. They often discussed different investment opportunities and worked on strategies together, constantly exchanging ideas.

The poor man felt grateful to the rich man for his act of kindness, and he knew the trajectory of his life had changed forever. With his newfound wealth, he could now help others in need, just like the rich man had helped him.

To cut the story short, the poor man's life had changed dramatically after the offer from the rich man. His financial independence had brought him a sense of comfort and security that he never thought possible. Through the unlikely friendship between two men, they learned and grew together, and both their lives were enriched for the better

# CHAPTER SIX

## LIVING THE DREAM

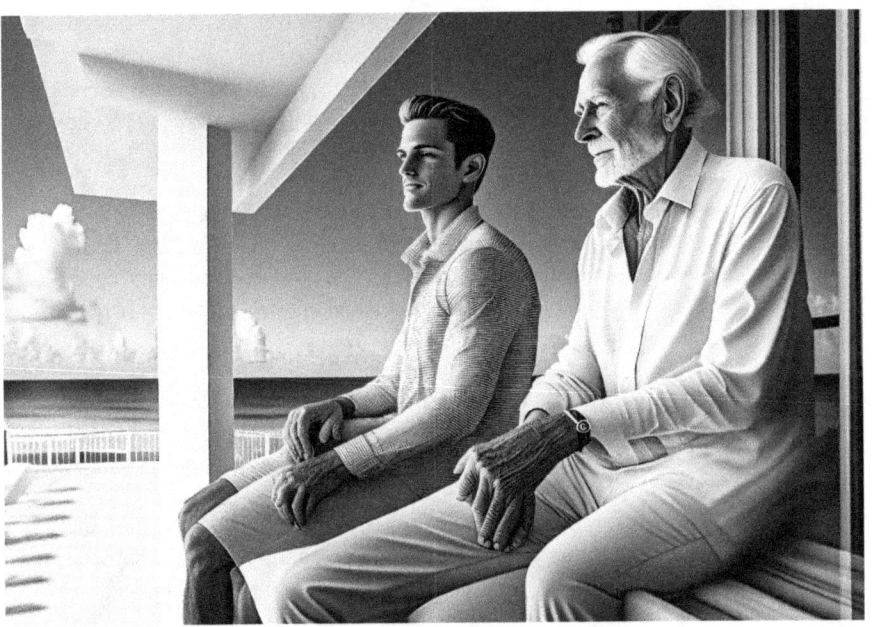

Living the Dream

Mr Alex and John sat on the balcony of their Miami Beach condo, watching the sun set over the ocean. They had made it. They were now living the life they had always dreamed of.

When they first met, John was broke and desperate to find a way out of his situation. Mr Alex was successful but lonely, looking for someone to pass on his knowledge and skills to.

They both had something that the other needed, and over time, they realized that they had more in common than they thought. They became friends and started collaborating, with John soaking up everything Mr Alex had to teach him.

The changes in their perspectives and attitudes towards each other were remarkable. John saw Mr Alex not just as a mentor but as a father figure who had helped him achieve his goals. Mr Alex, on the other hand, saw John as a partner and equal, capable of achieving anything he put his mind to.

Now, with their business flourishing, they looked back at their journey together with gratitude and appreciation. They had learned the power of mentorship and sharing knowledge to empower people.

As the sun disappeared over the horizon, Mr Alex turned to John and said, "You know, I never thought that I would find someone like you. Someone who was not only willing to learn but also to teach me new things."

John smiled and replied, "Likewise, Mr Alex. I never imagined that I would find someone who would believe in me and invest so much time and energy into making sure I succeeded."

They both raised a toast to a bright and prosperous future, knowing that it was their bond of friendship and commitment to mentorship that had brought them to where they were today.

The message was clear. With the right mentorship and the willingness to learn, we can achieve anything we set our minds to. We need to empower each other and pay it forward, just as Mr Alex had done for John.

They both knew that the road ahead would be challenging, but with each other's support, anything was possible. They were living the dream, a dream made possible by their friendship and mentorship.

# CONCLUSION

In conclusion, "The AI Investor: A Tale of Two Men" is a unique journey into the world of artificial intelligence and its impact on the investment industry. The story follows two men, one who relies solely on human analysis and the other who incorporates AI technology into his investment strategy. Through their experiences, readers gain an understanding of the potential benefits and challenges of using AI in investing.

Overall, the book highlights the importance of embracing innovation in an ever-changing world. It doesn't suggest that AI will replace human analysis, but rather it emphasizes the potential for AI to enhance and complement human skills. The book encourages investors to explore the possibilities of incorporating AI into their investment strategies, and to do so with caution, utilizing the expertise of both man and machine.

"The AI Investor: A Tale of Two Men" serves as a reminder that technology is constantly advancing, and we must be willing to adapt and evolve in order to remain competitive in the investment industry. Ultimately, the choice of whether to incorporate AI into investment strategies is up to each individual investor, but this book provides a valuable insight into the opportunities and challenges that AI presents.

THE END